80 Graded Studies for Clarinet

selected and edited by John Davies and Paul Harris

Book One (1–50)

CONTENTS

Faber Music Limited
London

This edition © 1986 by Faber Music Ltd
First published in 1986 by Faber Music Ltd
3 Queen Square London WC1N 3AU
Music engraved by Lincoln Castle Music
Cover design by M & S Tucker
Cover photography by Jason Shenai
Printed in England by Caligraving Ltd

INTRODUCTION

In the two books comprising this collection, we have assembled a broad repertoire of study material that covers the entire spectrum of basic technique and provides a firm foundation for progress. The studies have been arranged in order of increasing difficulty, according to a carefully planned technical progression. Book One begins at elementary level, while Book Two takes the student from intermediate to advanced level.

In the main, we have drawn on established study collections by distinguished performers of the 19th century, all of whom made an approach to the diverse problems encountered in the development of technical facility and control. We have also included a number of new, specially composed studies that introduce aspects of 20th-century style and thus extend the scope of the selection.

It is important to identify – perhaps with the assistance of your teacher – the specific purpose of each study and the particular facets of technique it sets out to develop. The following suggestions will be useful.

Breath control Most aspects of tonal control depend on a sustained and concentrated column of air. This is the basis of all *legato* and *staccato* playing, and a means of controlling intonation.

Tone quality It is important to maintain quality and consistency of tone when playing studies, scales and technical exercises.

Dynamics While the actual volume of sound implied by particular dynamic markings may vary from work to work, dynamic relationships within a single study should be constant. *Crescendo* and *diminuendo* should always be carefully graded, increasing or decreasing at a constant rate.

Intonation When practising studies, it is important to test intervals by reference to a tuning fork, piano or electronic tuning device.

Articulation The chosen length and quality of notes should be matched throughout and related to the character of the particular study. An understanding of the various symbols used is necessary.

Finger technique The development of a controlled and coordinated finger movement is the main purpose of the technical study. You should always identify the particular difficulties and seek to acquire the necessary control.

Rhythm These studies should often be practised with a metronome. Where there are rhythmic difficulties, sub-divide the basic pulse. You should always count, but it is important that undue emphasis is not placed on beats, except for a slight feeling for the natural bar accents. These primary and secondary accents should be felt but not over-emphasized.

Character The character and mood of a study should be considered, as these will determine note duration, accentuation, tone-colour and so on.

Metronome markings In most cases we have indicated the *maximum* tempo for each study. You should use your discretion regarding suggested metronome marks.

Breathing indications These are suggestions and need not be strictly observed.

JOHN DAVIES
PAUL HARRIS
1986

For detailed guidance on all aspects of technique, see *Essential Clarinet Technique* by the same authors.

LIST OF SOURCES

The studies in these books are drawn from the following sources:

Carl Baermann (1811–1885)
Vollständige Clarinett-Schule (André, 1864–75)
(39, 53, 73)

Frédéric Berr (1794–1838)
Méthode Complète de Clarinette (Meissonnier, 1836)
(18, 42)

Friedrich Demnitz (1845–1890)
Clarinetten Schule (Breitkopf & Härtel)
(1, 5, 9, 12, 13, 16, 19, 21, 22, 23, 25, 27, 34, 35, 47, 52)

Hyacinthe Klosé (1808–1880)
Méthode Complète de Clarinette (Meissonnier, 1843)
(28, 61, 65)

Henry Lazarus (1815–1895)
New and Modern Method (Lafleur, 1881)
(15, 33, 38, 41, 44, 55, 56)

Jean Xavier Lefèvre (1763–1829)
Méthode de Clarinette (Paris Conservatoire, 1802)
(32, 66)

Iwan Müller (1786–1854)
Méthode pour la nouvelle clarinette (Gambaro, 1822)
(51, 62, 63, 68, 76, 78)

Cyrille Rose (1830–1903)
40 Studies (Carl Fischer)
(54, 57, 58, 59, 70, 71, 74, 77)

Robert Stark (1847–1922)
Practical staccato school, op. 53 (Benjamin, 1909)
(2, 3, 24, 26, 31, 36, 40, 45, 50)

Amand Vanderhagen (1753–1822)
Méthode nouvelle pour la clarinette (Boyer et Lemenu, 1785)
(46)

Ludwig Wiedemann (1856–1918)
69 Studies (Breitkopf & Härtel)
(29, 43, 48, 64, 69, 72, 75, 80)

GLOSSARY OF TERMS

Accelerando	Becoming gradually faster
Adagio	Slow
Allegro	Lively
Allegretto	A little slower than *Allegro*
Andante	*lit.* 'at a walking pace'
Andantino	A little faster than *Andante*
Assai	Very
A tempo	Resume the original speed
A piacere	*lit.* 'at the pleasure of the performer' *(ad lib.)*
Ben	Well
Cantabile	In a singing style
Con	With
Da capo	From the beginning
Dolce	Sweetly
Duolo	Grief
Energico	Energetically
Espressivo (espr.)	Expressively
Fine	End
Furioso	Furiously
Fuoco	Fire, spirit
Larghetto	Somewhat slowly
Legato	Smoothly
Leggieramente	Lightly
Maestoso	Majestically
Marcato	Marked
Meno mosso	Less movement
Moderato	At a moderate pace
Morendo	Dying away
Non troppo	Not too much
Più	More
Poco	Little
Poco a poco	Little by little
Presto	Fast
Quasi	As if
Rallentando (rall.)	Becoming gradually slower
Risoluto	Resolute
Ritardando (rit.)	Becoming gradually slower
Secco	Dry
Sempre	Always
Simile	In the same manner
Sostenuto	Sustained
Staccato	Short and detached
Stringendo	Pushing forward
Tempo di marcia	In the time and style of a march
Tenuto	Held
Vigoroso	Vigorously
Vivace	Lively
Vivo	Vigorous

f = forte (loudly)
p = piano (softly)

80 Graded Studies for Clarinet

1

Friedrich Demnitz

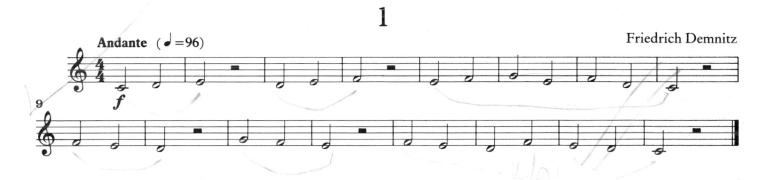

2

Robert Stark

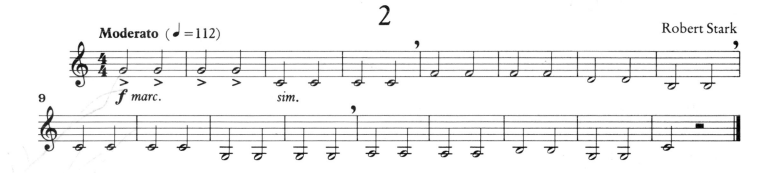

3

Robert Stark

4

Paul Harris

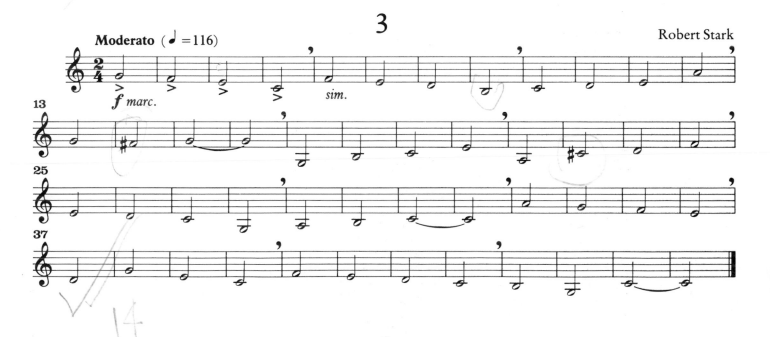

5

Andante ($\bullet$ =108)

Friedrich Demnitz

6

Moderato ($\bullet$ =120)

Paul Harris

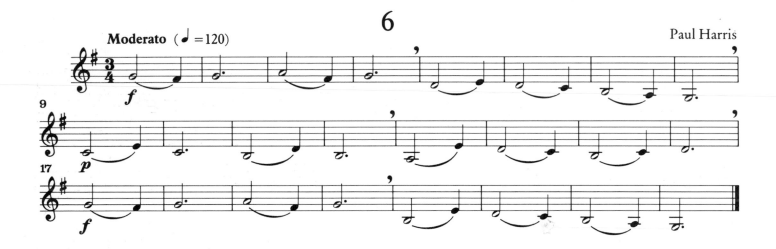

7

Adagio ($\bullet$ =72)

Paul Harris

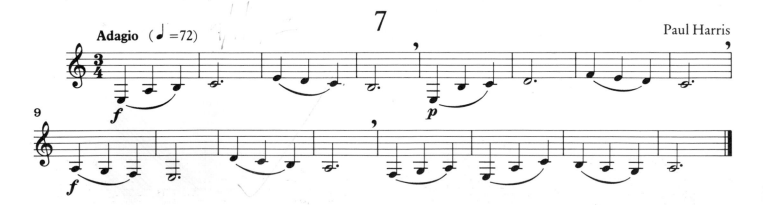

8

Moderato ($\bullet$ =112)

Paul Harris

9

Con moto (♩=126)

Friedrich Demnitz

10

Andante (♩=108)

Paul Harris

11

Moderato (♩=120)

Paul Harris

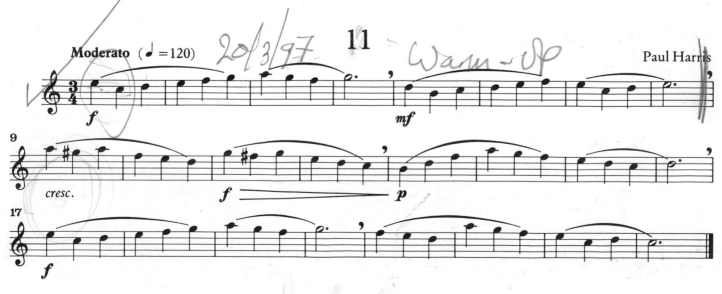

4

15

16

17

6

18

Andante (♩=112)

Frédéric Berr

19

Moderato (♩=126)

Friedrich Demnitz

20

Allegretto (♩=116)

Paul Harris

21

8

24

Andante (♩=104)

Robert Stark

25

Moderato (♩=120)

Friedrich Demnitz

26

Moderato (♩=126)

Robert Stark

9

27

Allegro moderato (♩ = 132)

Friedrich Demnitz

28

Allegro (♩ = 126)

Hyacinthe Klosé

29

Shepherd's Song – Hirtenlied

Allegretto con moto (♩ = 116)

Ludwig Wiedemann

10

30

Allegretto con moto (♩=112)

Paul Harris

31

Allegretto (♩=108)

Robert Stark

32

Moderato (♩=138)

Jean Xavier Lefèvre

33

Henry Lazarus

34

Friedrich Demnitz

35

Friedrich Demnitz

36

Andante (♩ =112)

Robert Stark

37

Allegro (♩ =120)

Paul Harris

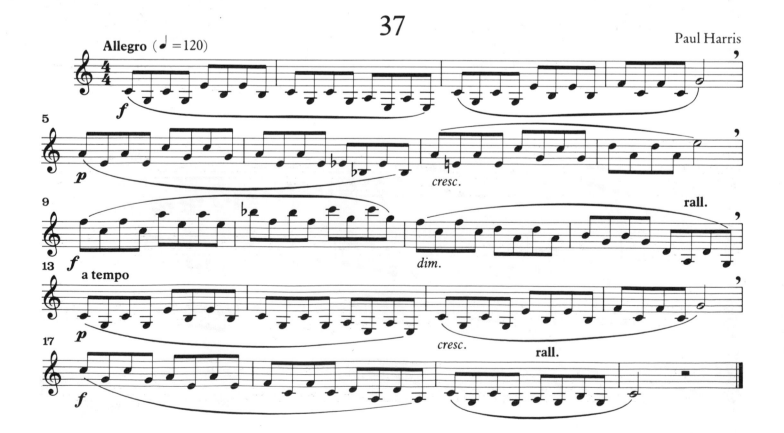

38

Henry Lazarus

39

Carl Baermann

14

40

41

42

Allegretto (♩=126)

Frédéric Berr

43

Mazurka

Ludwig Wiedemann

Allegro con fuoco, quasi presto (♪=138)

44

The Turn – Der Doppelschlag

Henry Lazarus

45

Robert Stark

46

47

48

Csardas

Ludwig Wiedemann

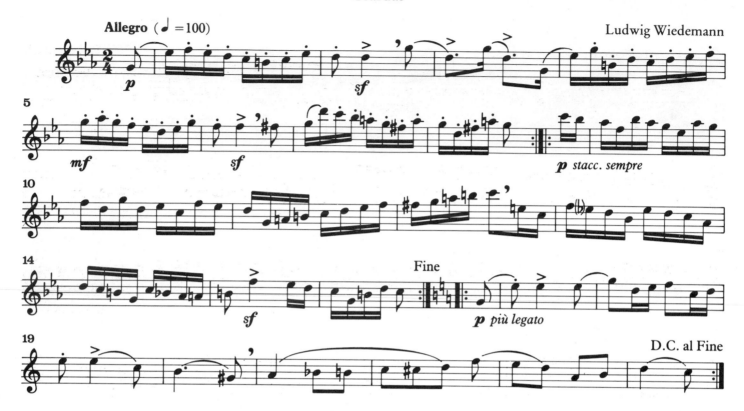

49

Paul Harris

50

Robert Stark